BRITAIN IN OLD PHO

MARYLEBONE &
PADDINGTON

R I C H A R D   B O W D E N

WESTMINSTER CITY ARCHIVES

ALAN SUTTON PUBLISHING LIMITED

Alan Sutton Publishing Limited
Phoenix Mill · Far Thrupp · Stroud
Gloucestershire · GL5 2BU

First published 1995

Copyright © Richard Bowden and Westminster
City Archives, 1995

Cover photographs: (front) Paddington station,
c. 1892 (see p. 100); (back) King Alfred public
house yard, 1904 (see p. 105).

British Library Cataloguing in Publication Data.
A catalogue record for this book is available from
the British Library.

ISBN 0-7509-0907-2

Typeset in 9/10 Sabon.
Typesetting and origination by
Alan Sutton Publishing Limited.
Printed in Great Britain by
WBC, Bridgend, Glamorgan.

To the memory of my parents

Traffic congestion just north of Marble Arch, *c.* 1900. The east/west boundary between Marylebone and Paddington ran down the middle of Edgware Road and Maida Vale, while Bayswater Road and Oxford Street formed the southern boundary. On the left is the corner of Connaught Place. This was the site of Tyburn gallows.

Contents

Westbourne Grove at the turn of the century, looking towards Queensway. Before William Whiteley opened his first shop here in 1863, Westbourne Grove was known as 'Bankruptcy Row'. However, within ten years, Whiteley had made his name and Westbourne Grove was established as a shopping centre.

Feeding the ducks in Regent's Park, *c.* 1900. Some things never change.

Introduction

Everyone has heard of Oxford Street and Paddington station, Lord's and Madame Tussaud's. They are what might be called the public face of Marylebone and Paddington, familiar to every Londoner and foreign visitor. Their more private side is only fully known to the people who live there, but these photographs, which go back more than 100 years, show something of both the public and the private sides of the two communities.

A generation has now passed since Marylebone and Paddington became part of the City of Westminster in 1965. Although they are no longer separate metropolitan boroughs, they still have quite separate identities, for the history of each area is very different. Marylebone is Georgian, building having begun in around 1720 in Cavendish Square, but Paddington did not begin to take its present form until nearly a century later, well after the arrival of the Grand Junction Canal in 1801. Both, however, had been villages since medieval times and smaller settlements for many hundreds of years before that.

The derivation of the name Marylebone in itself tells a story. Marylebone's first parish church, St John's, was probably founded in the thirteenth century. It was in Oxford Street, at the corner with Marylebone Lane, but rather too close to Tyburn gallows. The problem of vandalism was so serious that, in 1400, this church had to be closed. A new one, dedicated to St Mary, was built in a more secure place near the top of what is now Marylebone High Street, opposite the manor house and well away from Oxford Street. As this church was close to Tyburn stream, the village became known as Maryburn or Marybourn, the form Marylebone becoming established by about 1700.

There is sometimes confusion about whether or not Marylebone should have the prefix 'St'. 'St Marylebone' was always used by the civil as well at the ecclesiastical parish and this was why it was retained after 1900 by the borough council. Today the prefix is much less used. Marylebone High Street, Marylebone station and the Marylebone Cricket Club, to take three instances, have never included it.

Paddington's first parish church also dated back probably to the thirteenth century and its site was near that of the present St Mary's church. The early village was here, close to where Harrow Road meets Edgware Road. The Westbourne stream, which flows south from Kilburn through Hyde Park, formed part of Paddington's western boundary, and there was another small village, Westbourne Green, just beyond it. The southern boundary of Marylebone and Paddington was along Oxford Street and Bayswater Road, and the east–west boundary between them was Edgware Road, all of them formerly Roman roads.

Once building had started progress was very rapid. In Marylebone, houses had spread north to Marylebone Road by 1800 and Regent's Park and St John's Wood were fully built up by 1860, the whole process taking less than 150 years. Paddington was developed even more quickly, also from south to north, starting at Connaught Place, near Marble Arch. The pace of its growth was one reason for the poor quality of some of the housing. The last area of Paddington to be completed was Maida Vale, in around 1910.

Both Marylebone and Paddington include a number of well-known features of national significance – London's first underground railway, the Grand Union Canal and Regent's Park, for example. Photographs of as many of these as possible have been included in the book, together with a cross-section of pictures from different parts of each former borough.

All the photographs are from the extensive collection now at the City of Westminster's archives centre, where anyone interested can see them. Each of the former boroughs had their own local history collection and considerable additions have been made since 1965 by purchase, donation or bequest. There are now some 20,000 photographs of Marylebone and Paddington in the collection. The wealth of choice meant that a large number of excellent photographs simply could not be included in the book.

The selection I have made relies on two groups of photographs in particular. First, the range of postcards of street scenes, which were produced before 1914, both well-known and obscure streets being represented. The number of different views of some streets is remarkable: the collection has, for example, eighteen different views of Harley Street from that period. They are a wonderful resource and more of them are added to the collection every year.

The second notable group consists of the photographs taken in the 1950s and 1960s, by members of the St Marylebone Society and the Paddington Society. These two local societies were founded in 1948 and 1957 respectively, and are still in existence. They presented these photographs to the libraries of the former boroughs, and they form a marvellous record of the two areas at that time. The late Mr Basil Green and Mr Edward White both took hundreds of photographs of Paddington, many of them outstanding pictures, while the St Marylebone Society's annual photographic competitions, which were held from 1949 to 1964, produced work of a professional standard. Many of the entries for these competitions were also given to the library.

This selection is drawn particularly from both these groups but it includes material from a wide range of sources. Some of the photographs included here have been used in exhibitions within Westminster but most of them have never been published before.

Richard Bowden, 1995

STREETS AND
BUILDINGS

The view east along Oxford Street from Selfridges, about ten years after it opened in March

1909. In the eighteenth century, apart from various places of entertainment, including a

boxing establishment, Oxford Street was residential, but it has been a shopping street now

for more than 100 years.

The north side of George Street, looking west from Durrant's Hotel, Manchester Street, c. 1920. Much of Marylebone is Georgian, planned and built from about 1760 onwards, and large numbers of its Georgian houses still survive.

Nos 8–18 Edgware Road, close to Marble Arch, in 1903. The executions at Tyburn gallows are thought to have been witnessed from the first-floor windows of the house on the right of this picture. Public executions were held at Tyburn for 600 years, ending in 1783. The Odeon cinema occupies this site today.

Marylebone Circus, the junction of Marylebone Road and Baker Street, soon after the Bakerloo line was built in 1906. Baker Street station dates back to 1863, when the Metropolitan Railway, the world's first underground line, was opened, running from Paddington to Farringdon Street. Even at this early date London's streets remained busy, in spite of the underground railways. Madame Tussaud's can be seen in the background.

St Marylebone parish church from York Gate, almost 100 years after it was built. Designed by Thomas Hardwick and completed in 1817, it replaced the old parish church, which had become too small for Marylebone's enormously expanding population. The old parish church is seen below in 1948. By this time it was in a damaged and dangerous state and, in 1949, it was demolished. The unusual memorial garden, which is on its former site today, incorporates many of the tombstones from the old church and churchyard, including that of Charles Wesley, the great hymn writer and evangelist, who lived nearby.

Marylebone High Street, *c*. 1920. The High Street, whose origins are probably medieval (p. 5), is Marylebone's oldest inhabited street, although now there are no buildings left in it from before about 1750. In 1668 Pepys came here – with a lady friend – to visit the Marylebone Gardens, which were just to the east of it.

Harcourt House, Cavendish Square, in 1904. Until 1906, when it was demolished, this mansion occupied the whole of the west side of Cavendish Square. Here Robert Harley, 2nd Earl of Oxford, began to develop his Marylebone estate in 1717. The high walls around the house were built by its last owner, the eccentric 5th Duke of Portland, whose father won back the lease of the house in a game of cards.

St James's church, Westmoreland Street, shortly before its demolition. The National Heart Hospital was built on this site. The last vicar of this church was the Revd Hugh Haweis, described as one of the greatest preachers of his day. The church was pulled down soon after his death in 1901.

Baker Street, north of Portman Square, in Edwardian days. St Paul's church, on the right of the picture, was damaged during the Second World War and later demolished. There are very few original houses left in Baker Street, but no. 109, near York Street, is the kind of house that Conan Doyle's no. 221B was based on.

Regent Street with All Souls' church, Langham Place, at the turn of the century. The architect John Nash created Regent Street to link Carlton House with Marylebone Park. He also designed All Souls' church, which was completed in 1824. Its circular portico leads the eye round towards Portland Place.

Oxford Street, looking west from Duke Street, in the mid-1880s. Queen Street, on the left, was renamed Lumley Street in 1886. Twenty years later Selfridges replaced the houses on the right.

The Hope Tavern, on the corner of Glentworth Street and New Street, now Melcombe Street, in 1898. These small streets were laid out in around 1810 as service streets for the large houses near Dorset Square. Within five years of the date of this picture Clarence Gate Gardens were built.

The south side of Melcombe Street, looking towards Baker Street, *c.* 1900. These houses were demolished when Berkeley Court and Dorset House were built, in 1928 and 1935 respectively. Racing at Ascot is the main item on the newspaper headlines in the picture.

Lisson Grove, *c.* 1910. Spencer, Turner and Boldero was a large wholesale drapers, whose main premises were just north of Ashmill Street. It closed in the 1960s after over 120 years of trading. Lisson Grove is full of interesting associations; for example, Shaw's Eliza Doolittle came from here.

A group of houses in Bell Street in the 1950s. Bell Street is nearly 150 years older than most of the streets around it, having been associated with the old coaching inns in the Edgware Road. In the background is Christ Church, Cosway Street.

St John's Wood High Street in 1900, before the days of boutiques, estate agents and motor cars. The High Street dates from around 1820, when the area was first developed. Many of these houses are still there today, including the Duke of York public house.

Carlton Hill, St John's Wood, at the junction with Greville Road, in 1900. A tranquil, almost rural scene, epitomizing the attraction of St John's Wood as a place to live both then and now. The small spire belongs to the Carlton Hill chapel.

Hanover House and Northgate with the Portland Arms public house, near St John's Wood burial ground, in 1900. These huge Victorian blocks were the first flats to be built on this scale in St John's Wood. Many more followed as the original long leases came to an end in the 1920s, greatly changing the character of the area.

The junction of Harrow Road and Edgware Road (above), soon after they had featured in the Jack Warner film of 1950, *The Blue Lamp*. With the opening of Westway in 1970 many local landmarks disappeared from here, including Paddington Town Hall (p. 50) and the Metropolitan Theatre (pp. 64–5). Marylebone flyover, shown below during its construction, was opened by the Greater London Council in October 1967.

Maida Vale, looking north, *c.* 1910, when it was still lined with comfortable family houses on both sides.

Delaware Mansions, one of the many blocks of mansion flats in Maida Vale, soon after its completion in 1908. The BBC's Delaware Road studio was originally built, in 1912, as a roller-skating rink.

Westbourne Terrace with Holy Trinity church, Bishop's Bridge Road, *c.* 1955. Westbourne Terrace was the centrepiece of the group of terraces running north from Bayswater Road, which were planned and built mainly in the 1840s. To the left is one of the blocks of the controversial Hallfield estate, built by Paddington borough council after this area had been seriously damaged during the war. Sir Denys Lasdun, architect of the Royal National Theatre, was closely involved in its design. Holy Trinity church was demolished in 1985, the building not having stood the test of time. The railway can be seen in the distance, with puffs of smoke from the steam trains.

Part of Bayswater Road, with Lancaster Gate, *c.* 1910. These magnificent terraces facing Hyde Park were designed in 1856–7 by the architect Sancton Wood. They were built as private apartments but today are hotels.

Queensway, *c.* 1900, with the United Methodist Free Church, now the church of Our Lady, Queen of Heaven. Queen Victoria used to come riding here as a child from Kensington Palace. After her accession its old name, Black Lion Lane, was changed to Queen's Road, changing again to Queensway in 1937.

The Lodge, Porchester Square, not long before the site was cleared, in 1913, to build Paddington's new public baths, now known as the Porchester Centre. From 1885 the house belonged to Sir Henry Charles Burdett, KCB, editor of *The Hospital*, and he may well be the figure in the picture practising on the croquet lawn.

Porchester Road, looking north from Bishop's Bridge Road, *c.* 1910. The new public baths were only completed in 1925, and Porchester Hall in 1929.

Porchester Road, looking south from Westbourne Park Road, *c.* 1910. The greatest change here since then is not so much the look of the street as the traffic.

The church of St Mary Magdalene in 1960, during the redevelopment of the Warwick estate. The streets in the semi-circle between the canal and Harrow Road became overcrowded soon after they were built in the 1850s; their redevelopment after 1957 by the LCC, and later the GLC, was long overdue. This church was designed by G.E. Street, architect of the Law Courts, and completed in 1878.

Lothrop Street, Queen's Park, *c.* 1910. The popular and well-run Queen's Park estate was an independent development, in 1875, by the Artizans, Labourers and General Dwellings Company, which remained its landlords until 1964 (see also p. 42). The turret at the end of the street is a typical feature of this estate.

St Mary's church on Paddington Green, *c.* 1910. A church is first mentioned in Paddington in 1222, and the present church, which dates from 1791, is probably the third on this site. As Paddington's population spiralled upwards, St Mary's became too small and, in 1845, St James's, Sussex Gardens, became the parish church.

Section Two

CHILDREN

The children of St Mary's, Bryanston Square Church of England school in June 1907,
after winning first prize for their presentation 'The Empire's Premiers' at a London
festival. England, Ireland, Scotland and Wales are in the centre of the group.

Two pictures taken outside 531 Wharncliffe Gardens, Lisson Grove: above, Norman and George Andrew in their pram in 1898; and, below, a group of children in 1903 in their Sunday best, including Billy Mavin, Cyril and Elsie Kirby, Hertop Jones and the two Andrew boys. Between 1981 and 1983 their brother, Ronald, published *The Wharncliffe Gardens Story*, an excellent and entertaining account of the community he had grown up in.

The classroom of St Marylebone Charity School for Girls in 1895. The school was founded in 1750 to educate poor and needy children in the parish in domestic work, and it continued in existence until 1934. In the 1890s the school was in Marylebone Road, opposite the parish church, where the Royal Academy of Music is today. Originally it took boys as well as girls, but after a rebellion by the boys in 1828 ended in them all being expelled, it was for girls only. This is one of a set of photographs of the school taken in the mid-1890s. The girls are working on a long division sum on their slates. The classroom has bare boards but it is roomy and well equipped, with a ceiling fan and all sorts of teaching aids. It is difficult to see whether the cage contains a parrot or a guinea-pig. Perhaps it was for the next lesson.

Two more photographs of St Marylebone Charity School in 1895 – the laundry (above) and the kitchen (below).

The fourth form of St Marylebone Grammar School in 1910, with their form master, Edwin Frisby and the school Sergeant and Drill Master, A.H.F.L. Cramer. The Grammar School was at the junction of Marylebone Road and Lisson Grove. It was founded in 1792 as the Philological School and closed in 1981 (see also p. 37).

The photograph on the left shows an elegantly posed group of girls from Queen's College, Harley Street, in 1904. The first school in the country devoted to the higher education of women, it was founded in 1848, and is still in existence at 46–8 Harley Street. The writer Katherine Mansfield was one of the pupils at the school at this time. In the photograph on the right children from St Michael's Church of England school, Star Street, play outside the school in the late 1950s. Before the Second World War there was a special class here for canal-boat children. This school closed in the early 1970s.

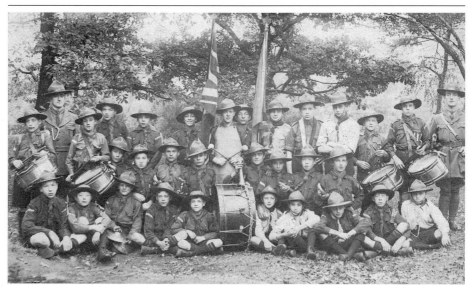

The 21st St Marylebone Scout Troop, *c.* 1915.

A cheerful group of girls from the St Marylebone Church of England school in Marylebone High Street, playing at the back of the parish church, *c.* 1910. This school goes back over 200 years to 1791, when it was founded as a National School.

Children playing in Providence Place, Lisson Street, just before its demolition in 1926.

May Day at All Souls' Church of England school, Foley Street, in 1956.

Hopscotch in Queen's Terrace, St John's Wood, in 1951. Behind the children is All Saints' church hall, where the first St John's Wood library was opened in 1947. All Saints' church was demolished in 1978.

Section Three

WORK

A chairmender in St John's Wood, 1951.

Robert Miller outside the family smithy at 34 Bell Street, in 1900. He is holding the horseshoe tongs and with him are some of his sons, who helped in the forge.

Labourers working in Hyde Park, *c*. 1902.

A group of St Marylebone Grammar School teachers in 1888–9. From left to right: back row, Mr Wolfsberger, Charles Houseman, Mr Knowles, Mr Cumberland and Edward Morant; front row, Mr Kitz and Mr Moore. The school kept its original name, The Philological School, until 1901.

Benjamin Warsop and Son's cricket-bat factory, at 127A Park Road, *c*. 1914, is shown in the photograph on the left. 'Cricket bat maker to the principal players of England', this firm closed in 1975 after almost 100 years in St John's Wood. The 1872 photograph on the right shows 'Young Mary', one of the milkmaids from William Stoat's Alderney Farm Dairy, which was in Gloucester Place, near the junction with Marylebone Road.

Mrs Hunt's Agency, at 86 Marylebone High Street, *c.* 1910. This was an employment agency mainly for servants, who were a major part of London's workforce before the First World War.

Regent Street with flower girls, *c.* 1910. The public conveniences here were opened in 1892. The shop on the right in this crowded scene is Peter Robinson.

A picture dating from *c.* 1915. This shop is still at 105A Crawford Street. It looks much the same today, though it is now called Meacher, Higgins and Thomas. The figure on the left is Gwilym Thomas, who came to London in 1913. He took over the business five years later and was succeeded by his son, who still owns it.

Manchester Square fire station in Chiltern Street, c. 1910. This handsome fire station was built by the LCC in 1889, and is little changed today – apart from the horses. The numerous fires at Whiteleys during the 1890s would have been fought by its firemen.

The interior of Webster and Girling, a theatre ticket agency in Upper Baker Street, probably about 1905. It included a public telephone call office, which, to judge by this picture, was well used.

Two photographs from an unusual series of twelve which were taken during the construction of the new Westbourne Terrace Road bridge over the canal at Little Venice, in 1900. In the second picture a horse is crossing the bridge, perhaps to show that it really was successfully finished.

Van drivers from D.H. Evans, *c.* 1920. A horse can just be seen in the background too, so the vans must have been very new. This store was founded by Dan Harries Evans, a Welshman from Llanelly, who opened a lace and dress shop in Oxford Street in 1879, assisted by his wife and other members of his family.

The maintenance staff of Queen's Park estate, in the late 1940s (see also p. 26).

A travelling knife-grinder in Brown Street, behind Seymour Place, in 1963.

A study in contrasts in Abercorn Place, *c.* 1960. A dog guards a busker's mobile gramophone, while parked behind them is a Rolls Royce.

The employment exchange at 211 Marylebone Road, beside the church of Our Lady of the Rosary, in 1953. The new employment office in Lisson Grove opened four years after this.

A street trader selling nylons in Oxford Street, in 1952.

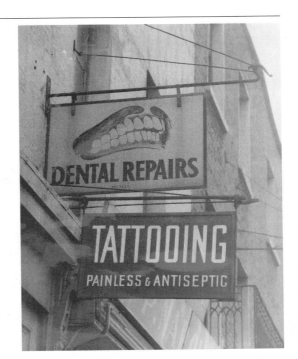

No. 43 Praed Street, in 1959. As well as the tattoo artist and the dental repair service, there were five other businesses at this address in 1959: a tool importer, a photographic company, a china dealer, a dressmaker and a dealer in artists' materials. Office space as well as housing was evidently still in short supply.

A home-made mobile shop in Paddington, 1961.

The steps of the convent of St Vincent de Paul, Blandford Street, *c.* 1960. The large numbers of Irish immigrants during the nineteenth century are an important element in the Catholic communities of both Marylebone and Paddington. St James's church in George Street, near here, built in 1890, replaced the Spanish embassy chapel which gave its name to Spanish Place. It dated back to 1791.

Section Four

LOCAL AFFAIRS

The council chamber of Paddington Town Hall, 1900. Changes in London's local
government structure led to both Marylebone and Paddington becoming metropolitan
boroughs in that year.

North Wharf Road, during the North Paddington parliamentary election of October 1900. T
were two constituencies in Paddington then, north and south. The gentleman with the beard i
John Aird, who was MP for North Paddington from 1887 to 1905. In 1900 he also bec
Paddington's first mayor.

The pavilion built for the opening of Paddington Recreation Ground on 9 July 1890, by HRH The Prince of Wales. As can be seen, it was a wet day. It took almost twenty years of patient campaigning by R. Melvill Beachcroft, secretary of the Paddington Cricket Club, to secure this open space as a public amenity.

Harrow Road with, on the left, Paddington Town Hall, *c.* 1910. Built in 1853 by James Lockyer as Paddington's vestry hall, the Town Hall stood beside Paddington Green. It had to be demolished in 1965 to make room for Westway.

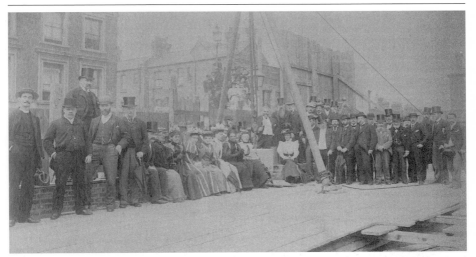

Laying the foundation stone of Kensal Road baths, in August 1896. Curiously, until 1900, Kensal Town and Queen's Park formed a detached portion of the parish of Chelsea. These baths were therefore built by the vestry of Chelsea but, together with Queen's Park library, they passed to Paddington borough council in 1900.

Councillor Leonard Snell, mayor of Paddington, laying the foundation stone of Porchester Hall on 29 October 1927. Beside him is the lady mayoress, his daughter, Guinevere. The Porchester Hall development was the brainchild of Sir William Perring MP, chairman of the Baths Committee. It was designed by the architect Herbert Shepherd.

A lunch for 150 guests, given at Porchester Hall by Alderman Sir William Perring, on 26 September 1929, as part of its official opening. Paddington's Turkish and Russian Vapour baths and new public library were included at the same opening ceremony.

Wilcove Place, Church Street in 1915 (see also p. 79). Lord Portman, who then owned this part of Marylebone, had agreed to reconsider his plans to demolish this street – clearly a popular decision. The street was eventually pulled down in the early 1930s by St Marylebone Housing Association, and replaced by the Wilcove estate (see p. 121).

Two pictures of the Cart Horse Parade in the Inner Circle of Regent's Park, *c.* 1900. This was an annual event which first took place in 1886. In 1966 it was amalgamated with the Van Horse Parade, a similar but separate annual event, which started in 1904. Since then it has been called the Horse Harness Parade. It still takes place on Easter Monday in Regent's Park.

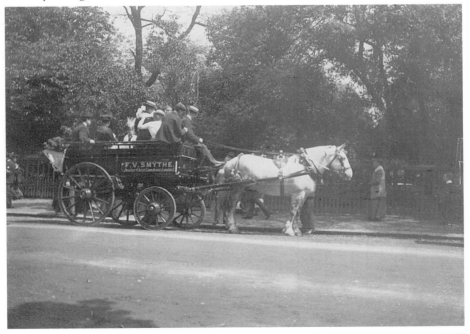

An etching by Norman Janes in 1948 of St Marylebone Town Hall and public library. Both buildings were designed by the architect Sir Edwin Cooper but are twenty years apart in date. The Town Hall (now Westminster Council House) was completed in 1920 and Marylebone library in 1940. A public library was first opened in the basement of the Town Hall in 1923.

James Wilson being presented with a motor cycle and sidecar on his retirement in 1924, after twenty years' service as Town Clerk of St Marylebone. He is standing in the centre of the photograph. On his right is his successor, Leslie Gordon. On the extreme left of the picture, in the wing collar, is Duncan Gray, first borough librarian of St Marylebone.

Councillor Gregory Matveieff, Mayor of St Marylebone, greeting HM the Queen Mother at the Royal College of Midwives, Mansfield Street, in March 1961. In the background is his macebearer, Mr Matthews, who retired in the 1970s after over forty years' service with St Marylebone borough council, and then Westminster City Council.

Councillor Charles Press, mayor of St Marylebone, at the opening of the new Women's Voluntary Service headquarters at 104 St John's Wood Terrace, c. 1950.

Posters for the LCC election of April 1961. It looks as if Eva Bartok was part of Labour's election campaign.

The closing ceremony for Luxborough Lodge on 6 January 1965 with Lord Hailsham, then Quintin Hogg, MP for St Marylebone. This was an historic moment – Luxborough Lodge, previously known as the St Marylebone Workhouse, dated back to the eighteenth century. The Polytechnic of Central London, which is now the University of Westminster, was built on this (Marylebone Road) site.

SOCIAL LIFE, SPORT AND THE PARK

A garden party given by Viscountess Portman at Montagu House, Portman Square,

in July 1898, when 'a very smart and fashionable crowd took tea and discoursed scandal

under the trees'.

Madame Tussaud's not long before the fire of 1925. This destroyed some, although not all, of the oldest items in the exhibition. Today Madame Tussaud's is still London's leading tourist attraction. Madame Tussaud herself came to England in 1802 and opened her first permanent exhibition in Baker Street in 1835. The collection moved to its present site in 1884.

Hertford House, Manchester Square, soon after it opened the Wallace Collection to the public in 1900. This fabulous private collection includes paintings, furniture, armour and china. The house itself, which was originally built by the 4th Duke of Manchester because of the excellent local duck shooting, dates back to 1776.

Sir Henry Wood conducting the orchestra of the Royal Academy of Music in June 1936. He devoted two afternoons per week to this. The Royal Academy of Music moved to Marylebone Road in 1912.

The Queen's Hall, Langham Place, c. 1905. Sir Henry Wood started his promenade concerts here in 1895, two years after it was built. The 'proms' were transferred to the Albert Hall after a direct hit destroyed the Queen's Hall in 1941. Part of All Souls' church can be seen on the left.

Porchester Hall, with Paddington's new public library, soon after it was opened in 1929. There were plans in the 1950s to build a new Paddington civic centre here, south of Porchester Square, but they did not come to fruition.

Inside Porchester Road library, *c.* 1938. The range of headgear is interesting.

The reading room at Queen's Park library, *c.* 1905. This library was built by the parish of Chelsea in 1890, ten years before Queen's Park became part of Paddington. It was Paddington's only public library until 1923, when a small library was finally opened in Hatherly Grove.

A visit to Portman Square by members of the St Marylebone Society in July 1949, the year after the society was founded (p. 6). The speaker is Cecil Smith, ARIBA. The mayor of St Marylebone, Councillor Charles Press, is standing slightly right of centre, wearing his badge of office. The ladies' hats here are magnificent.

The Eyre Arms in the late 1920s. This well-known centre of local entertainment used to be at the corner of Grove End Road and Finchley Road. It was built in 1820, with its own assembly rooms. The view of St Paul's from its roof was an additional attraction. It was demolished to build Eyre Court in 1929.

T.C. Dorrell, left, landlord of the Richmond Arms, Orchardson Street, *c.* 1924, with a *News of the World* darts champion. The table of trophies with the dart board itself must have been moved out into the street especially for this photograph.

The Langham Hotel, photographed on 4 July 1898. The tiny, horse-drawn delivery cart standing in front of it, dwarfed by the building, is marked 'American Express Co'. The Langham was built in 1864. After the Second World War it was used for some years by the BBC, but was restored and reopened as a hotel in 1991.

A billiards saloon at 48 Praed Street in 1911, when billiards was one of the few popular and widely accessible entertainments.

Edgware Road near Church Street, with the 'Met', in 1963, the year it was demolished. This famous theatre dated back 100 years, taking its name from the Metropolitan railway. It was said to be haunted by the ghost of a manager who was killed on active service in France during the First World War.

METROPOLITAN
EDGWARE ROAD

Manager—W. GENEVER

Ambassadors 2478

6-30 • MONDAY, AUGUST 10th, 1959 • 8-45

THE FABULOUS
TESSIE O'SHEA

FOLLOWING HER U.S.A. & CARIBBEAN TOUR

WITH **ERNEST WAMPOLA**

Acclaimed as one of the World's Greatest Modern Pianists

DESEVIA
INTERESTING MAGICIAN

PETER

DANCING **HOLLANDS**

PETER NOVELTY BOX
RAYNOR

FIVE FAST AND FURIOUS
LOMBARDS

JIMMY TARBUCK
YOUR YOUNG HOST

MAXWELL
PIANO PLAYBOY

BILL THE RURAL RUSTIC
GILES

A variety programme from August 1959, with some names that are still familiar today. The theatre was used for boxing and wrestling, and even as a television studio, towards the end of its life.

The staffroom of St Marylebone Charity School for Girls in the 1890s. The comfortably cluttered Victorian interior includes an aspidistra in the corner of the room (see pp. 29–30).

The interior of a luxury apartment in Hyde Park Terrace, *c.* 1920. There is, unfortunately, no record of who owned it. The ornate plasterwork, fine panelling and valuable china and books certainly all indicate a wealthy owner.

The lady cyclist seems to be very much taken for granted as she pedals along the Harrow Road in the early years of the century. The Neeld Arms public house, at the junction with Marylands Road, still looks the same today. The Neeld family were responsible for developing a small grid of streets here, behind the Harrow Road.

Cyclists in Regent's Park, 1900.

The start of a cycle race at Paddington Recreation Ground in 1888 between Mr Du Cros and Mr Macredy. It was the first race in which Dunlop pneumatic tyres were used. This was before the raised cycle track was built, which has recently been removed.

Out for a stroll in Regent's Park in 1900. When it was first completed, in the 1920s, the park was open only to its residents but by as early as 1841 most of it had been fully opened to the public.

An attractive litter of King Charles spaniel puppies outside York Terrace, Regent's Park, in 1938.

The dogs' cemetery at Victoria Gate, Hyde Park, *c.* 1910. This cemetery was started in 1880 by the Duchess of Cambridge, whose husband was ranger of the park. The last burial was in 1915.

The Zoological Society was founded in 1824 and opened its gardens in Regent's Park to the public two years later. The zoo was always extremely popular. The captions on these two Edwardian postcards are both playfully ambiguous: above is 'The Lion House', although not a lion is to be seen, while the picture below is captioned simply, 'The parrots at the zoo'.

A camel ride at the zoo in August 1913.

This photograph of the keepers of Regent's Park was presented to J.B. Sowerby, secretary of the Royal Botanic Society, in 1898. The Royal Botanic Society occupied the Inner Circle of Regent's Park from 1839 to 1931, and J.B. Sowerby was the third generation of his family to be associated with it.

A ladies' archery competition in Regent's Park, in 1901. For ninety years, up to 1922, the Royal Toxophilite Society leased the five acres where the tennis courts are now. Archery contests can sometimes be seen today in Kensington Gardens.

A performance of Shakespeare's *Pericles* at the Open Air Theatre in Regent's Park, in 1940. The Open Air Theatre was founded in 1932 by Sydney Carroll, and is still a major summer attraction, weather permitting.

The public baths in Marylebone Road, shortly before the new ones in Seymour Place were built in 1936. The handsome Victorian façade of the Marylebone Road baths, including the foundation stone, have survived – the building was taken over by the Marylebone Magistrates' Court, which is still there today.

These two photographs look older than they are. They show the lunch interval during the Eton and Harrow match at Lord's, in July 1934. Thomas Lord opened his first cricket ground on the site of Dorset Square in 1787 and this was where the Marylebone Cricket Club was formed in the same year. The first Eton and Harrow match was played here in 1805. By 1809, however, as the Portman estate expanded northwards, the ground had to move. A new site was found at North Bank in St John's Wood

but Lord's did not reach its present home until 1814, after a further move. On each occasion Thomas Lord moved the turf with him. In 1896 when the Great Central Railway was building its line to Marylebone – in the teeth of vociferous opposition from local St John's Wood artists and residents – the turf was removed before the tunnel was built under the ground and carefully replaced afterwards. The Eton and Harrow match is still an annual fixture at Lord's.

Marjory Usher and her brother, Harry, setting off from 49 York Terrace, *c.* 1937, to be presented at Court.

Tennis in Regent's Park in 1923. This photograph shows a charity match arranged by Lady Wavertree in aid of the Invalid Children's Aid Association. W. Johnson (USA) and S. Lenglen (France) are playing V. Lycett and Miss Ryan. The match was at Sussex Lodge, which was demolished in 1959.

Section Six

PUBLIC EVENTS

Sir John Aird, Mayor of Paddington, with the borough councillors, waiting at Paddington

station to welcome Lord Kitchener on his return from South Africa in 1902.

Two photographs taken at the unveiling of the statue to the actress Mrs Siddons, on Paddington Green, by Sir Henry Irving on 14 June 1897. The statue is by Leon-Joseph Chavalliaud. Mrs Siddons was associated with both Marylebone and Paddington, having lived at Westbourne Farm from 1805 to 1817 and then in a house at the top of Baker Street, overlooking Regent's Park, from 1817 to her death in 1831. She is buried in Paddington. The lower picture shows Frank Dethridge, Vestry Clerk and the Honorary Secretary of the Statue Committee, greeting the guests.

Marylebone High Street decorated for the coronation of King Edward VII, in 1902.

A group photograph taken in Wilcove Place in 1902, at the time of the coronation of King Edward VII (see p. 52).

Paddington and Marylebone both organized particularly lavish entertainments for the children of their respective boroughs to celebrate the coronation of King George V on 27 June 1911. A huge party for 12,556 children was held at Paddington Recreation Ground, while all the Marylebone children were taken out to Wembley Park for the day.

The finish of a keenly contested race during the 1911 coronation celebrations at Wembley Park.

The annual St Marylebone Borough Council banquet held on 22 June 1904 in the Hotel Great Central. This had been completed five years earlier, along with Marylebone station. After being used as the headquarters of British Rail after the Second World War, it reopened as a hotel – The Regent – in February 1993. Happily, almost all its sumptuous internal decoration has survived.

The review of the London Division of the National Reserve in Hyde Park by King George V, in June 1912. In the foreground, the mayor of one of the London boroughs is bowing to the Queen and Princess Mary.

A communist demonstration passing Marble Arch, *c.* 1925. Speakers' Corner is just across the boundary with the former City of Westminster. The right to free assembly here was won as long ago as 1872, so there is a long tradition of marches and demonstrations.

The Silver Jubilee of King George V and Queen Mary in 1935. Huge crowds are waiting in Baker Street for the royal procession.

The band of the Grenadier Guards at St John's Wood Barracks during an inspection of the London District Headquarters of the Royal Corps of Signals by Princess Elizabeth on 25 June 1941.

The King's Troop, Royal Horse Artillery, crossing Bryanston Square on their way from St John's Wood Barracks to Hyde Park, to fire the salute on the birth of Prince Andrew, on 19 February 1960.

The coronation of Queen Elizabeth II took place on 2 June 1953. The photograph above shows a coronation street party in the Bourne Terrace area of Paddington, and the one below, the decorations in Walmer Street, Marylebone.

Section Seven

SHOPPING

The entrance to Whiteleys, at the corner of Porchester Gardens and Queensway, soon after 1911, when this impressive new building was completed. The store was forced to close in 1981, but a shopping and leisure centre has since been opened here, using the same premises (see p.4).

The north side of Westbourne Grove, at the corner with what is now Chepstow Road, *c.* 1910. Arthur's Stores was one of the many shops that flourished here when Whiteleys was enjoying such success. The house to its left was, for forty years, the home of one of Paddington's more unusual residents, Prince Louis Lucien Bonaparte, a nephew of Napoleon. He became a philologist of some distinction and died here in 1891.

Allsep Bros, a florist and fruiterers at 12 Craven Road, close to Paddington station, *c.* 1910.

Praed Mews, off Norfolk Place, in 1911. This mews is similar to many others in this part of London. The pair of ladders belonged to W.H. Smith, builder and decorator, of 12 London Street, and the long wooden seat must have been thoughtfully provided by the restaurant round the corner for its customers.

Market stalls in Great Titchfield Street, *c.* 1905. This photograph is looking south from Langham Street. The Oxford Market, at the southern end of Great Titchfield Street, had been closed for about thirty years.

The boys' outfitting department on the first floor of Peter Robinson's, at Oxford Circus, probably about 1920. Peter Robinson was a Yorkshireman who came to London in 1833, and opened a draper's shop on part of this Oxford Street site. The business was taken over by Burton's in 1946 and eventually closed in 1986.

Two smart young shoppers outside Gayler and Pope, at the corner of Blandford Street and Marylebone High Street, in 1902. This small-scale but popular local department store survived until 1958.

This photograph dates from 20 April 1904, and is one of a large group of good-quality photographs which were taken for insurance purposes when the Bakerloo line was being built. W Hirons' newsagent and tobacconist shop was on the east side of Carlisle Street – renamed Penfold Street in 1937 – near the corner with Bell Street. The little boy on the left has a cigarette in his right hand.

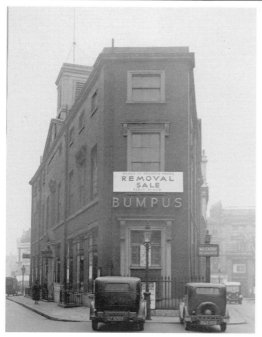

Two photographs of J. and E. Bumpus, a large Oxford Street bookshop. Their premises were then at 350 Oxford Street, the former St Marylebone watch house, at the southern end of Marylebone Lane, where the Earl of Oxford had built his court house in 1729. In time this became the parish vestry house, and, until 1920, Marylebone's Town Hall. The photograph above was taken in 1935, when Bumpus had reached the end of their lease and were moving to another Oxford street site. The lower photograph shows the ground floor of the bookshop in 1930.

The first floor of the Oxford Street bookshop, in 1894. John Wilson, who was manager of Bumpus from 1921 to 1959, was a leading figure in the London book world, corresponding with many contemporary authors such as T.S. Eliot, Vita Sackville-West and T.E. Lawrence. At his retirement he was made an OBE.

The branch of Marks & Spencer at 228 Edgware Road, soon after it opened in 1922. Ten new Marks & Spencer branches were opened in London that year. Above the 'Admission free' notice can be seen the penny symbol.

Dubowski's Stores at 136 Church Street, on the eve of its opening, probably in 1922. Like his friend Jack Cohen, and many others, Dave Dubowski started with a stall in Petticoat Lane.

The interior of Dubowski's Stores, again *c.* 1922. On the left is a tempting display of chocolates and sweets. The rest of the shop is full of groceries, with plenty of butter and eggs. You almost feel you are in the shop.

Church Street market. The photograph above was taken in 1955 and the one below, showing the south side of the street, in 1953. The white porch in the centre of the lower picture was the entrance to the former West London Theatre, which was bombed in 1941 and demolished in the 1960s, to make way for a new housing development.

No. 545 Harrow Road, probably *c.* 1953, as meat rationing ended in the following year.

No. 121 Westbourne Grove in 1961. One hopes that at least some of John Dennis's eight children were able to earn their own living.

St Christopher's Place, 1954. In the eighteenth and nineteenth centuries this alley was a notorious slum called Barrett's Court. In 1877 it was renamed by Octavia Hill, founder of the National Trust, while she was supervising its renovation. Above the shop-fronts, on the west side, the figure of St Christopher, which was placed there at that time, can still be seen. In the past ten to fifteen years St Christopher's Place has been smartened up and, in the process, it has changed completely.

Section Eight

TRANSPORT

The Marylebone parish steamroller, a ten-ton Aveling and Porter model, c. 1893.

The canal tow-path in use at Blomfield Road, *c.* 1900. In the background is the Catholic Apostolic church, Maida Avenue, which was designed by the architect J.L. Pearson and completed in 1893.

The canal-boat *Buffalo*, which was used by three generations of the Stanton family from Paddington. Here it is thought to be moored beside an ice merchant at Amberley Wharves, in or around the year 1900. Mr Stanton is the second figure from the right in the picture. Not long ago *Buffalo* was seen on the canal system, still in use.

Paddington Basin in 1953. One or two of the buildings in this photograph date back to the early part of the nineteenth century. The Grand Junction (now the Grand Union) canal was extended to Paddington in 1801, and the Paddington Basin was, for some time, an important terminus for London's trade with the Midlands.

Narrow boats moored at Little Venice, *c.* 1958.

Above, Paddington station, *c.* 1892, looking towards the buffers of platforms 1 and 2. Its famous roof, inspired by the Crystal Palace at the Great Exhibition of 1851, was designed by the great engineer Isambard Kingdom Brunel, assisted by Matthew Digby Wyatt and Owen Jones. Brunel's broad gauge was used on the Great Western Railway up to 1892. In this photograph the additional track needed for standard gauge trains can be seen. This was introduced at Paddington station in 1861, three years after Brunel's death. Below, a friendly engine driver and fireman, *c.* 1960, just before steam trains disappeared for ever.

Above, Marylebone station within a year or two of its opening in 1899. How the photographer persuaded this group of businessmen to pose for him will never be known. Every single one of them is wearing a hat! Marylebone was the terminus for the Great Central Railway, the last line to London to be built. Below, the 12.15 express for Manchester just moving off in 1958.

The *Master Cutler* about to leave the turntable just outside Marylebone station, 1958. The line to Marylebone was originally planned by the Manchester, Sheffield and Lincolnshire Railway company, hence the regular express service to Sheffield and its distinctive name.

The Marlborough Road underground station, *c.* 1905. This was a Metropolitan line
station at the junction of Queen's Grove and Finchley Road. It closed in 1939 and for
many years the building has been a Chinese restaurant.

Bleriot's aeroplane at Selfridges. On 25 July 1909 Louis Bleriot became the first man to
fly the English Channel. The very next day his aeroplane was put on display in the
basement of Selfridges. Bleriot also had a local connection: he was the director of a
motor-lamp factory in Seymour Place.

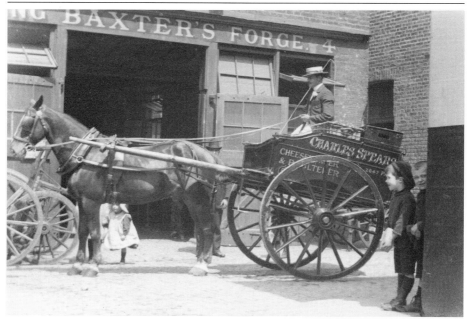

Cross Keys Mews behind Marylebone High Street, *c.* 1900, when blacksmiths were still a common sight in London.

Stable lads in Huntsworth Mews, Dorset Square, *c.* 1900.

The yard of the King Alfred public house, Lisson Grove, in 1904, graphically demonstrating one aspect of life at that period. Part of St Edward's convent can be seen behind the yard.

The entrance to a livery stables in Ordnance Hill, *c.* 1905. Up to about 1920 London had numerous livery stables. If you were not in a position to keep your own horse and carriage at home, this was where you could hire one.

A horse and cart in Harrow Road, near Cirencester Street, *c.* 1910.

Varied traffic in Park Road, near St John's Wood parish church, *c.* 1905. The statue of St George and the Dragon by the sculptor Charles Hartwell was presented to the borough by Sigismund Goetze in 1936 (see p. 124), and erected here as a war memorial.

The junction of New Street, now Melcombe Street, and Baker Street, *c.* 1925, when no one imagined that parking would ever be a problem. This terrace was demolished in 1928.

A garage at 2 Great Central Street, *c.* 1920.

The south side of Portman Square from Wigmore Street, *c.* 1920. The lack of traffic islands and street signs makes it difficult to recognize where this is. Also, this side of the square has been completely redeveloped since then.

Traffic in Marylebone Road at the junction with Gloucester Place, *c.* 1930, when the site of Dorset House was being cleared for its construction. There does not really seem to be any need for the policeman on point duty.

Section Nine

WAR

HM Queen Elizabeth visiting the Paddington 103rd Nursing Division in 1945.

The 36th Middlesex Paddington Rifle Volunteers, known as the Paddington Rifles, *c.* 1875.

Foot inspection of members of 'F' Company, 3rd City of London Battalion, the London Regiment, at Perham Down Camp, Wiltshire, in 1913.

Kitchener's Army in Regent's Park, during the summer of 1914. Above, recruiting in the rain: the notice reads, 'St Marylebone, your country needs you'. Below, basic training.

A 1918 party in Carlisle Street (now Penfold Street), Lisson Grove, to celebrate the end of the First World War.

The unveiling of the war memorial in St Marylebone Town Hall, in July 1921, by the Bishop of Birmingham, Dr Russell Wakefield, a former mayor of St Marylebone. This memorial is to members and staff of the council.

The war memorial to the people of Queen's Park and St Peter's Park, at the junction of Beethoven Street and Herries Street. This memorial, which was unveiled in around 1921, has recently been moved to the wall of Sloman House, on the Mozart estate.

A Paddington ARP exercise at the corner of Dart Street and Herries Street, *c.* 1939.

St Marylebone Fire Patrol team 'A' at the Town Hall in 1939.

Bomb damage to the north side of Oxford Street in April 1941, near Newman Street, looking east.

The one that missed the BBC . . . This is the view from Broadcasting House looking towards Langham Street and Hallam Street, showing the destruction caused by a bomb which fell there in April 1941. Broadcasting House was not damaged.

Two of the 'mechanized midwifery squad' of Queen Charlotte's Hospital in 1940, the year the hospital moved from Harcourt Street to Hammersmith. As well as the steel helmets that these midwives are wearing for their personal protection during the Blitz, a special anti-shrapnel device was fitted to the roof of the cars they used.

During the summer of 1942, as part of the war effort, St Marylebone public library manned this small lending library in Regent's Park. It was open from 2.30 p.m. to 6 p.m. every day except Sundays, and one book at a time could be borrowed for up to seven days.

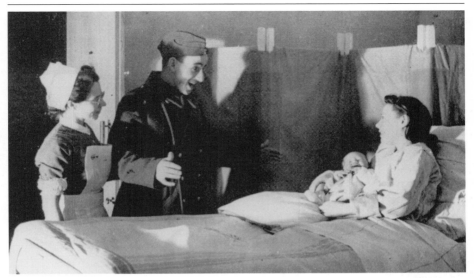

Queen Charlotte's Hospital published this photograph in 1940 with the caption, 'A fighting man greets his son'.

War savings publicity in Paddington Street, 1942.

A military parade at St Marylebone Town Hall, probably in 1942.

A children's party to celebrate VE Day at Tadema House, Church Street, during the summer of 1945.

Section Ten

PEOPLE

Mozart Street from Bravington Road, c. 1910.

A street musician outside 7 Queensway, c. 1955.

A London street junkshop, 1960.

The junction of Lord Hill's Road and Senior Street, c. 1955, just before the major redevelopment of that area.

This photograph is thought to show the interior of a house in Wilcove Place, just before its rebuilding. It was taken for the St Marylebone Housing Association, *c.* 1930.

Penfold Street in 1956.

One of the two prize-winning horses entered in the Van Horse Parade of around 1905 by Mr Shurety, foreman of the Royal Mail stables in Taunton Place, Dorset Square. Several of his twelve children – nine sons and three daughters – are included in this photograph, which was taken in Gloucester Place, on their way home.

'Pay day' at the St Marylebone Almshouses, *c.* 1910. These almshouses are in St John's Wood Terrace. They were built in 1836 with money bequeathed by Count Simon Woronzow, the Russian ambassador to London during the Napoleonic War, who lived nearby. They were rebuilt in 1960 and are still very much in use.

Left, Charles Luck in 1960, celebrating his hundredth birthday at Porchester Hall and holding his telegram from the Queen. Right, Henry Parkes, who retired as gatekeeper in 1908 after working for the Royal Botanic Society for sixty-two years. He died in 1913 aged 83.

Left, the poet Robert Browning, who lived at 19 Warwick Crescent, overlooking Little Venice, from 1861 until his death in 1887. Right, Sir Rowland Hill, who lived at 1 Orme Square from 1839 to 1842, at the time when he was establishing the uniform Penny Post. He introduced the famous Penny Black postage stamp on 6 May 1840.

Left, Sigismund Goetze, artist, sculptor and local benefactor, photographed in 1904. He lived at Grove House, Regent's Park, now known as Nuffield Lodge, for thirty years from 1909. Right, W.E. Gladstone, who lived at 73 Harley Street, briefly in 1876. This photograph was taken in 1884.

Lord Hailsham, as Quintin Hogg, campaigning in Church Street market during the by-election of November 1963, when he was first elected MP for St Marylebone. He remained St Marylebone's MP until 1970, when he became Lord Chancellor.

The King Edward VII Hospital for Officers, Beaumont Street, in 1964. A group of reporters wait for news of former prime minister Harold Macmillan after an operation. This is a familiar scene in Marylebone which has several hospitals used by famous people. Today, however, reporters tend to gather in somewhat larger numbers, particularly if members of the royal family are involved.

Madame Marie Blanche of 66 Queen's Grove, St John's Wood, which was advertised as a French hand laundry, in 1955.

Jubilee party, Foley Street, 1977.

Acknowledgements

The following have kindly given their permission for particular photographs to be reproduced [(a) indicates the upper part of a page and (b) the lower part]:

Judith Cinnamond, p. 28 • Evening Standard, p. 60(b)
Mrs Doreen Fifield, p. 62(b) • Greater London Record Office, p. 56(b)
Hampstead and Highgate Express, p. 55(b) • *Illustrated London News*,
p. 59(a) • Imperial War Museum, p. 83(a) • Mr J.P. Kelleher, p. 110(b)
Kilburn Times, p. 42(b) • Mr E. McNeal, pp. 31(a) and 37(a)
Marylebone Mercury, p. 83(b) • Mrs Kathleen Miller, p. 36(a)
Marks & Spencer plc, p. 91(b) • Mr Victor Priddle, pp. 79(a), 88(b)
and 104(a) • Queen Charlotte's Hospital, pp. 115(b) and 117(a)
St Marylebone Housing Association, p. 121(a) • Mr Ernie Shurety, p. 122(a)
Mr G. Stanton, p. 98(b) • Mr Ivor Thomas, p. 39(b)
the Master and Fellows of Trinity College, Cambridge, p. 37(b) right
Miss M. Usher, pp. 69(a) and 76(a) and, in particular, Mr Tony Davies,
pp. 31(b) left, 32(b), 40, 42(a), 58(a), 72, 74–6, 87(b)
and 97

The generosity of the many other individuals and organizations who have presented photographs to Westminster City Archives or its predecessors is greatly appreciated. I should also like to thank all my colleagues at Westminster City Archives for their help and support while this selection of photographs was being compiled.

BRITAIN IN OLD PHOTOGRAPHS

To order any of these titles please telephone Littlehampton Book Services on 01903 721596

ALDERNEY

Alderney: A Second Selection, *B Bonnard*

BEDFORDSHIRE

Bedfordshire at Work, *N Lutt*

BERKSHIRE

Maidenhead, *M Hayles & D Hedges*
Around Maidenhead, *M Hayles & B Hedges*
Reading, *P Southerton*
Reading: A Second Selection, *P Southerton*
Sandhurst and Crowthorne, *K Dancy*
Around Slough, *J Hunter & K Hunter*
Around Thatcham, *P Allen*
Around Windsor, *B Hedges*

BUCKINGHAMSHIRE

Buckingham and District, *R Cook*
High Wycombe, *R Goodearl*
Around Stony Stratford, *A Lambert*

CHESHIRE

Cheshire Railways, *M Hitches*
Chester, *S Nichols*

CLWYD

Clwyd Railways, *M Hitches*

CLYDESDALE

Clydesdale, *Lesmahagow Parish Historical Association*

CORNWALL

Cornish Coast, *T Bowden*
Falmouth, *P Gilson*
Lower Fal, *P Gilson*
Around Padstow, *M McCarthy*
Around Penzance, *J Holmes*
Penzance and Newlyn, *J Holmes*
Around Truro, *A Lyne*
Upper Fal, *P Gilson*

CUMBERLAND

Cockermouth and District, *J Bernard Bradbury*
Keswick and the Central Lakes, *J Marsh*
Around Penrith, *F Boyd*
Around Whitehaven, *H Fancy*

DERBYSHIRE

Derby, *D Buxton*
Around Matlock, *D Barton*

DEVON

Colyton and Seaton, *T Gosling*
Dawlish and Teignmouth, *G Gosling*
Devon Aerodromes, *K Saunders*
Exeter, *P Thomas*
Exmouth and Budleigh Salterton, *T Gosling*
From Haldon to Mid-Dartmoor, *T Hall*
Honiton and the Otter Valley, *J Yallop*
Around Kingsbridge, *K Tanner*
Around Seaton and Sidmouth, *T Gosling*
Seaton, Axminster and Lyme Regis, *T Gosling*

DORSET

Around Blandford Forum, *B Cox*
Bournemouth, *M Colman*
Bridport and the Bride Valley, *J Burrell & S Humphries*
Dorchester, *T Gosling*
Around Gillingham, *P Crocker*

DURHAM

Darlington, *G Flynn*
Darlington: A Second Selection, *G Flynn*
Durham People, *M Richardson*
Houghton-le-Spring and Hetton-le-Hole, *K Richardson*
Houghton-le-Spring and Hetton-le-Hole:
   A Second Selection, *K Richardson*
Sunderland, *S Miller & B Bell*
Teesdale, *D Coggins*
Teesdale: A Second Selection, *P Raine*
Weardale, *J Crosby*
Weardale: A Second Selection, *J Crosby*

DYFED

Aberystwyth and North Ceredigion,
   Dyfed Cultural Services Dept
Haverfordwest, *Dyfed Cultural Services Dept*
Upper Tywi Valley, *Dyfed Cultural Services Dept*

ESSEX

Around Grays, *B Evans*

GLOUCESTERSHIRE

Along the Avon from Stratford to Tewkesbury, *J Jeremiah*
Cheltenham: A Second Selection, *R Whiting*
Cheltenham at War, *P Gill*
Cirencester, *J Welsford*
Around Cirencester, *E Cuss & P Griffiths*
Forest, The, *D Mullin*
Gloucester, *J Voyce*
Around Gloucester, *A Sutton*
Gloucester: From the Walwin Collection, *J Voyce*
North Cotswolds, *D Viner*
Severn Vale, *A Sutton*
Stonehouse to Painswick, *A Sutton*
Stroud and the Five Valleys, *S Gardiner & L Padin*
Stroud and the Five Valleys: A Second Selection,
   S Gardiner & L Padin
Stroud's Golden Valley, *S Gardiner & L Padin*
Stroudwater and Thames & Severn Canals,
   E Cuss & S Gardiner
Stroudwater and Thames & Severn Canals: A Second
   Selection, *E Cuss & S Gardiner*
Tewkesbury and the Vale of Gloucester, *C Hilton*
Thornbury to Berkeley, *J Hudson*
Uley, Dursley and Cam, *A Sutton*
Wotton-under-Edge to Chipping Sodbury, *A Sutton*

GWYNEDD

Anglesey, *M Hitches*
Gwynedd Railways, *M Hitches*
Around Llandudno, *M Hitches*
Vale of Conwy, *M Hitches*

HAMPSHIRE

Gosport, *J Sadden*
Portsmouth, *P Rogers & D Francis*

HEREFORDSHIRE

Herefordshire, *A Sandford*

HERTFORDSHIRE

Barnet, *I Norrie*
Hitchin, *A Fleck*
St Albans, *S Mullins*
Stevenage, *M Appleton*

ISLE OF MAN

The Tourist Trophy, *B Snelling*

ISLE OF WIGHT

Newport, *D Parr*
Around Ryde, *D Parr*

JERSEY

Jersey: A Third Selection, *R Lemprière*

KENT

Bexley, *M Scott*
Broadstairs and St Peter's, *J Whyman*
Bromley, Keston and Hayes, *M Scott*
Canterbury: A Second Selection, *D Butler*
Chatham and Gillingham, *P MacDougall*
Chatham Dockyard, *P MacDougall*
Deal, *J Broady*
Early Broadstairs and St Peter's, *B Wootton*
East Kent at War, *D Collyer*
Eltham, *J Kennett*
Folkestone: A Second Selection, *A Taylor & E Rooney*
Goudhurst to Tenterden, *A Guilmant*
Gravesend, *R Hiscock*
Around Gravesham, *R Hiscock & D Grierson*
Herne Bay, *J Hawkins*
Lympne Airport, *D Collyer*
Maidstone, *I Hales*
Margate, *R Clements*
RAF Hawkinge, *R Humphreys*
RAF Manston, *RAF Manston History Club*
RAF Manston: A Second Selection,
   RAF Manston History Club
Ramsgate and Thanet Life, *D Perkins*
Romney Marsh, *E Carpenter*
Sandwich, *C Wanostrocht*
Around Tonbridge, *C Bell*
Tunbridge Wells, *M Rowlands & I Beavis*
Tunbridge Wells: A Second Selection,
   M Rowlands & I Beavis
Around Whitstable, *C Court*
Wingham, Adisham and Littlebourne, *M Crane*

LANCASHIRE

Around Barrow-in-Furness, *J Garbutt & J Marsh*
Blackpool, *C Rothwell*
Bury, *J Hudson*
Chorley and District, *J Smith*
Fleetwood, *C Rothwell*
Heywood, *J Hudson*
Around Kirkham, *C Rothwell*
Lancashire North of the Sands, *J Garbutt & J Marsh*
Around Lancaster, *S Ashworth*
Lytham St Anne's, *C Rothwell*
North Fylde, *C Rothwell*
Radcliffe, *J Hudson*
Rossendale, *B Moore & N Dunnachie*

LEICESTERSHIRE

Around Ashby-de-la-Zouch, *K Hillier*
Charnwood Forest, *I Keil, W Humphrey & D Wix*
Leicester, *D Burton*
Leicester: A Second Selection, *D Burton*
Melton Mowbray, *T Hickman*
Around Melton Mowbray, *T Hickman*
River Soar, *D Wix, P Shacklock & I Keil*
Rutland, *J Clough*
Vale of Belvoir, *T Hickman*
Around the Welland Valley, *S Mastoris*

LINCOLNSHIRE

Grimsby, *J Tierney*
Around Grimsby, *J Tierney*
Grimsby Docks, *J Tierney*
Lincoln, *D Cuppleditch*